Exercise Is Fun

Running

This is the park.

I like running in the park.

I can run and run
and run.

3

Climbing

Look at the **wall.**

We can climb on the wall.

We can go up

and up and up.

Swimming

Look at the pool.

I can swim up and down the pool.

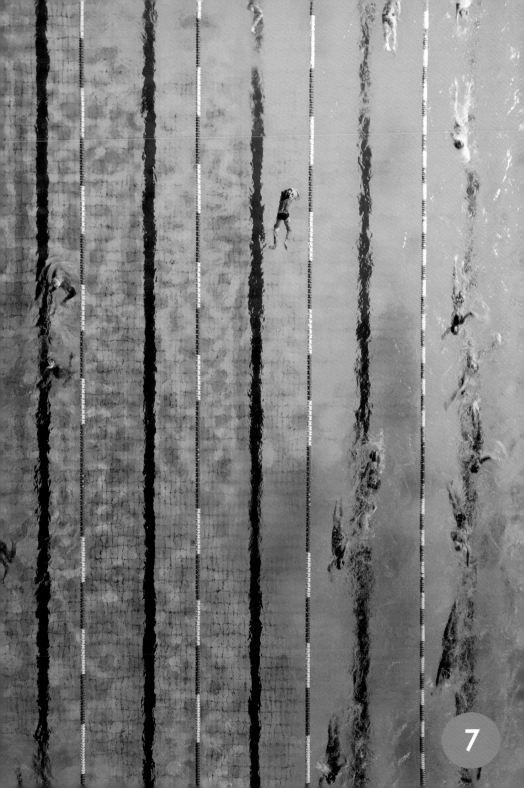

Crawling

I can go in the **tunnel** and come out the hole.

Kicking

Here is my ball.

I can kick my ball
to Dad.

Throwing

Here is my ball.

I can throw my ball.

My ball goes up, up, up!

13

Swinging

Look at me.

I can **swing** from hand to hand.